Fascination Series
A Curriculum and Planning Journal

PUDDLES

Fascination of Water
Nature-Based Inquiries for Children

By Dr. Claire Warden

Many thanks to the members of the Auchlone Kindergarten team, both past and present, for their contribution and in making this book possible.

Special thanks goes to all the children for whom we are in contact with on a daily basis for their joy and inspiration.

Photography by Claire Warden and the Kindergarten teams. All photographs ©Mindstretchers Ltd 2013. Image(s) used under license from Shutterstock.com:

Pages: 7, 10, 31, 40, 43, 44, 52, 60, 76, 81, 111, 112, 113, 114, 115, 116, 118, 119.

ISBN Paperback: 978-1-906116-59-0
ISBN Electronic: 978-1-906116-60-6

For further information about Mindstretchers publications and the full range of learning resources, email inquiries@mindstretchers.academy.

www.mindstretchers.academy

FOREWORD
By Sally York

Education Policy Advisor for Forestry Commission Scotland

You need time to play in puddles. It is one of those delights on a walk to discover a puddle and explore it: how deep is it, how wide is it, and how big a splash will it make? I love it when the puddles are frozen as the patterns are always different, and then there is the noise when you stand on the ice and it starts to fracture! The mud associated with puddles offers endless opportunities for "guddling" about. At the simplest level, just stomping through it, making patterns with your wellies, and, depending on the viscosity of the mud, seeing how long the patterns stay. "Mud, mud glorious mud" (otherwise known as "The Hippopotamus Song" by Flanders and Swann) sums up the pleasure of muddy puddles. Mind you, there are many times when it doesn't go near the sheer pleasure of mud!

Moreover, this is a very precious resource in life, not least when working with children. They need the time to explore the wonder of the world around them that, to tired adult eyes, can sometimes seem like messing about. It is this "messing about" that has such tremendous learning potential in many different ways and is essential for children, especially these days where their lives can be so driven by adult timetables.

There is a wonderful poem by W.H. Davies written in 1911 called "Leisure". It starts with: "What is this life if full of care we have no time to stand and stare". As adults, we have to make the time to "stand and stare" with children as they open up the endless possibilities of the world around them. It is in these instances that learning becomes child-led, but not just that; it can be that time stands still as we hark back to those initial fascinations we had as a child. It can open our eyes to the amazing world around us and allow us to see it through a child's eyes again. In my mind, there is nothing more important these days than to take the time to rediscover the fascination of something like "guddling" in puddles with a child to realize what is important in this world.

This book is a fascination in its own right. It is a great way to expose puddles in the way we need to record our work with children. It is an even better way to rediscover the sheer pleasure of puddles. Take the time to "stand and stare" with young children around puddles and prepare to be amazed!

Contents

Introduction
To The Fascination Series

Welcome to this series of nature-based curriculum and planning journals which have a beautiful combination of theory, curriculum, and reflection. You will be able to confidently embrace a more planet-centered way of educating children through collecting and completing this unique series of books. They will:

- Improve planning by providing pages of hundreds of possibilities to talk about with children;

- Improve engagement through inquiry-based learning in the Floorbooks®;

- Improve the quality of time you and children spend outdoors, so they become the stewards of the planet in the future.

When we work with colleagues worldwide who want to develop their nature-based practice, they have a few challenges. These journals will give the guidance and support needed to move forward with your practice. Some questions we explore in this series include:

- What is nature pedagogy all about?

- How do I cover academics when I go outside?

- What do children learn when they play with materials?

- How do I keep children safe?

- How can I build my confidence in planning for nature-based experiences?

- How can I share the learning with children and families?

These journals are part of a much broader set of opportunities and training on the www.Mindstretchers.academy where you can collect training certificates in both nature pedagogy and inquiry-based work through the internationally acclaimed Floorbook® approach.

Introduction Puddles

Puddles are one of the most easily accessible materials that children can play with. They appear suddenly and can transform a walk through the park into a puddle jumping adventure full of playful learning moments.

We can view a puddle as a challenge when we are not dressed for wet weather, yet they offer many possibilities for play and learning when we put our gear on. In this green curriculum journal, you will read case studies of children who learned about math by measuring the size, number, and depth of puddles and then making bridges to cross them. We can create programs and individual home learning moments that inspire children to discover and learn following these child-led moments. Through the guided reading in these books and the experiences children engage in, you will be astounded by the learning that can emerge from just being outside. Letting go of many adult structured tasks gives children the space to put forward their ideas and theories. This creates a co-constructed approach where children's inquiries are at the heart of delivering the curriculum.

Adults need to be skillful when they work with children. In this green curriculum, we use the natural world as a context for play and learning, the location inside and outside the four walls of a building, and the provider of resources to create thousands of possibilities for children to learn not just about nature but also the core academics and how relevant they are. You will learn more about your skills and knowledge of the natural world, which you can use to improve your confidence and planet-centered teaching strategies.

Planning is a vital part of our work in care and education. Being intentional is guided in this series through group documentation books called Floorbooks®, which give us the evidence to create a progression in our programs.

The last sections explore the risk management process and how we can become aware of the hazards inside or outside. These pages have sections for you to complete about the puddles in your space, including what you will talk about with children to ensure we adults don't say NO to puddle jumping.

The information is all here, ready to go. Let the adventure begin to work together to support children to have the chance to explore the potential of a puddle.

Claire

Dr. Claire Warden

1
What is a Puddle?

A puddle is a small accumulation of liquid, usually water, on a surface. It can form either by pooling in a depression on the surface or by surface tension upon a flat surface. Puddles are usually created from rainwater or irrigation.

A puddle tends to be small enough for an adult to step across, shallow enough to walk through, and too small to traverse in a boat. Puddles can be a source of fascination for children, as well as attracting small wildlife!

There are many people who have used the word puddle to create new and interesting phrases that can lead to wonderful language work with children, such as 'puddle jumper', a name given for short duration flights between lakes on seaplanes, a 'puddle light' for the light at the bottom of a car door, and 'puddle suits' for the waterproofs worn by children.

Natural Puddles and Nature's use

Puddles in natural landscapes and habitats can indicate the presence of a spring. In medieval times, these natural springs were often 'helped' along by lining a depression with naturally occurring clay to create a feature, like a small round puddle or pond. Historical accounts worldwide often mention cultural respect for clean water, where each drop of water was used and considered valuable.

A massive variety of life can exist in a puddle of water. Some wildlife, like birds, use puddles as a drinking source for bathing, or in the case of some smaller life-like tadpoles, an entire habitat. Raised constructed puddles, such as birdbaths, are a part of many domestic and wildlife gardens as a garden ornament and 'micro-habitat restoration.

Small seasonal plants, grasses, and wildflowers can germinate with a small amount of water in the ground, which is just enough moisture to start germination. In environments such as the temperate north, where there is rain all year round, the fringes of the puddle can often be the area that is colonized by small grasses.

How are puddles formed and where do they go?

Water Cycle

Our planet is fortunate in that it has the capacity to recycle water by cleaning as much of it as possible. Water is delayed from entering the groundwater level, when there is a barrier to its flow to the sea level. Puddles are a holding point for water as they can last for minutes or days, depending on the soil's climatic conditions and nature.

The water cycle refers to the continuous exchange of water within the hydrosphere, or between the atmosphere, soil water, surface water, groundwater, and plants.

Water moves perpetually through each of these regions in the water cycle consisting of the following transfer processes:

- Evaporation from oceans and other water bodies into the air and transpiration from land plants and animals into the air,

- Precipitation from water vapor condensing from the air and falling to the earth or ocean,

- Run-off from the land and usually reaching the sea.

Most water vapor over the oceans returns to the oceans, but winds carry water vapor over land at the same rate as run-off into the sea. Over land, evaporation and transpiration contribute to its return. Precipitation during the year over land has several forms: in our temperate climate of Scotland, it falls most commonly as rain, snow, and hail, with some contribution from fog and dew. Water droplets in the air can refract sunlight to produce rainbows.

Water run-off often collects over watersheds flowing into rivers. Some of the water is diverted to irrigation for agriculture. Rivers and seas offer opportunities for travel and commerce. Through erosion, run-off shapes the environment creating river valleys and deltas, which provide rich soil and level ground for establishing population centers.

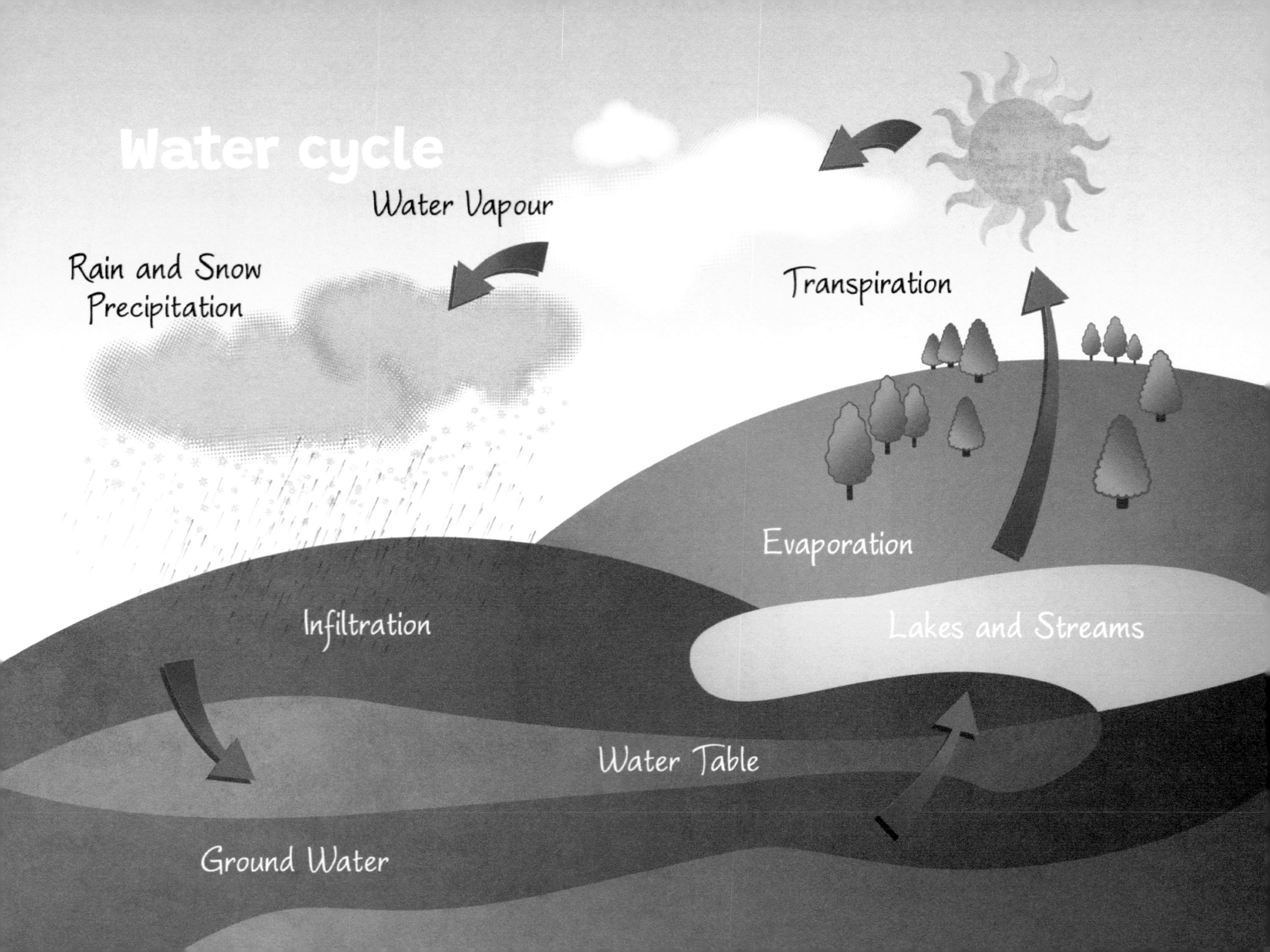

Water cycle

Water Vapour

Transpiration

Evaporation

Lakes and Streams

Water Table

Infiltration

Ground Water

Rain and Snow
Precipitation

Surface Tension

The most obvious element of a puddle is the surface and how it varies over a day, a week, or through the seasons. It is this feature that attracts attention before the shape of the outline as it reflects the light. Children find puddles exciting all year round. However, there are few people who can resist cracking the ice on puddles. Watching and hearing the ice crack while observing the muddy water seep up is a favorite aspect of going on long walks at the Nature Kindergarten.

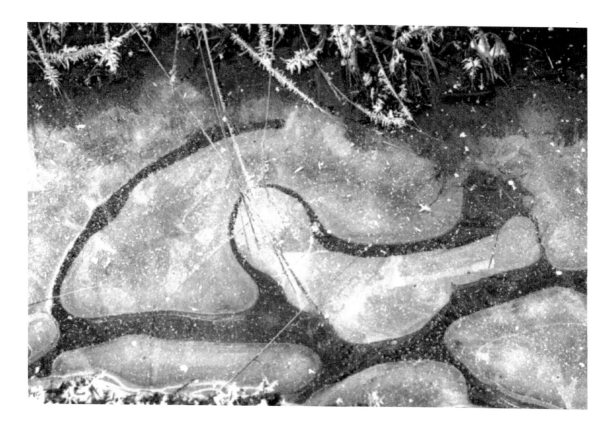

The cohesion of water molecules causes water tension. While the water molecules in the main body of the liquid are pulled equally by the other water molecules in every direction, the molecules at the surface of the body of water only have molecules pulling them downwards, creating surface tension.

The surface tension of a liquid is measured in something called dynes. The dynes required to break the surface tension of water is 72.

The existence of surface tension can be explored in many ways, from looking at water when it is in a clear container, observing a raindrop on a "Lady's Mantle" leaf, or floating objects on the top of the water, such as petals and grasses.

Fascinations Over the Years

Puddles are often a source of fascination by children, who regard jumping in puddles as an "up-side" to rain. A number of examples of this fascination are demonstrated in this book. The fascination for puddle exploration has been recorded throughout time. A good example of this is a children's nursery rhyme which records the story of Doctor Foster and his encounter with a puddle in Gloucester.

"Doctor Foster went to Gloucester In a shower of rain.
He stepped in a puddle Right up to his middle
And never went there again!"

The origins and history of the poem "Doctor Foster" are in the United Kingdom, and this is made clear with the reference to the southern county of Gloucestershire ("Doctor Foster went to Gloucester..."). The rhyme was a warning to children in bygone days, prior to modern roads, where what appeared to be a shallow puddle could, in fact, be much deeper!

A medieval legend originating from the UK spoke of one man who was desperate to find building materials for his house, so he stole cobblestones from the surface of the road. The remaining hole filled with water, and a horseman who later walked through the "puddle" actually found himself drowning. A similar legend is of a young boy drowning in a puddle that formed in a pothole in a major street in the early years of Seattle, USA, and is still told in areas of this region today.

When Walter Raleigh met Queen Elizabeth I, Raleigh is reputed to have thrown his coat over a muddy puddle to allow the Queen to cross without getting her feet wet. Such activities were once part of chivalry, but are less common nowadays!

Puddles have formed much fascination over the years for children and adults alike, so much so that a theory was devised known as "Puddle Theory" by Douglas Adams to satirize the "fine-tuned universe" argument for supernatural creationism. As quoted in Richard Dawkins' eulogy for Douglas Adams:

"...imagine a puddle waking up one morning and thinking, 'This is an interesting world I find myself in, an interesting hole I find myself in, fits me rather neatly, doesn't it? In fact it fits me staggeringly well, must have been made to have me in it!' This is such a powerful idea that as the sun rises in the sky and the air heats up and as, gradually, the puddle gets smaller and smaller, it's still frantically hanging on to the notion that everything's going to be alright, because this world was meant to have him in it, was built to have him in it; so the moment he disappears catches him rather by surprise."

This level of fascination with puddles and water appears to never truly leave us from early childhood to adulthood. It may be because puddles are an accessible area of water. In fact, because they are so common, we have lost the ability to see their potential.

In the poem on the next page, we can hear from a child the potential of a puddle:

Magic Puddles
by Lara Warden

Go on...

Jump In

Splash

Stir it

Race through it

Sit in it

Step over

Hop over

Leap over

Stand with your mum

Dance

Splish

Splash

Swish

Plop

Sing

Scream

Shout

Sigh

Look down under the water

Cover them

Find a friend

Find a bug

Twirl the water

Take measurements

Give it a name

Think about it

Watch it disappear

Make soup

Make perfume

Make a mess

Make a pond

Laugh And laugh

And giggle a LOT!

All of this... in a puddle.

In the Arts

Poems by adults have been written to stimulate a desire to jump in puddles, as well as describing the nature of puddles in relation to the water cycle. The following excerpt from the poem "The Lonely Puddle" by Wally Glickman demonstrates this wonderfully:

The Lonely Puddle
by Wally Glickman

Among all the lakes and the creeks and the brooks
and the streams and the rivers that water the valley
there lived a small pond,
no more than a puddle.
Rushing around her the others would babble
and clatter the pebbles and stones
and they'd giggle,
while she remained silent
and sad and alone.

Whenever the wind would arouse her to whisper
the others continued to pay no attention.
She'd stiffen her banks feeling angry and shy,
she'd clutch at her water, but never would cry.

The brooks and the streams always babbled of things
they had seen on their journeys,
they couldn't keep secrets.
They spoke of white snow on the peaks of high mountains,
they spoke of a lake that was known as the sea,
with waters so wide that it welcomed all rivers…
Just lies, thought the puddle, they're lying to me.

But oh how she listened and longed just to be
a small part of what gurgled and bubbled around her.
Why couldn't she be a brook or a stream
and glide over glistening pebbles and stones
instead of a puddle, apart and alone?

There is an abundance of children's literature and educational material available, including *The Puddleman* by Raymond Briggs (Jonathan Cape Ltd, 2004) and *Puddleman* by Ted Staunten (Kids Can Press, 1988).

The imagery of water expressed through literature, poetry, fine art, theatre, music, and film may be enduring, aesthetically appealing, or threatening. Additionally, water may be a metaphor for birth and rebirth, violence and death, self-discovery, spiritual journey, metamorphosis, change, inspiration, and renewal. Even small areas of water that are in a puddle offer enough stimulation that they catch our eye. The beauty of a still reflection can awaken a feeling of awe, and the murky depths of a muddy puddle can ignite a mind to consider "things" lurking in the murky depths.

Below are examples of artwork taken from the "Water" Floorbook® showing various children's impressions of water and puddles.

In ancient art, water was often represented by stylized curvilinear forms, such as the spiral or a horizontal zigzag (as found in the art of ancient Egypt). In the famed eleventh-century Bayeux Tapestry, the English Channel is represented by embroidered wavy black lines.

The brilliant Renaissance painter, sculptor, and inventor Leonardo da Vinci (1452–1519) was fascinated by water, which he described as "vetturale di natura" (the vehicle of nature). He drew it with great precision and fine detail, examined and studied it closely, was constantly in awe of its power from witnessing terrible floods and storms, and designed complex canal systems and locks to channel and control it.

The water world provides inspiration for folk art. Folk art is produced mostly by self-trained artists or for the preservation of traditional ethnic cultures, including functional and decorative hand-carved wildfowl and fish decoys, decorated sea chests, ship's figureheads, and nautical ornaments. In America, the zenith of traditional folk art flourished in the nineteenth century prior to the rise of industrialization. Traditional Vietnamese water-puppet performances continue a rich and ancient folk art theatre tradition in which the puppeteers stand behind a screen in water up to their waists with the floating bamboo water-puppet theatre occupying the middle of a pond.

Music

The arts encompass the environment of sight, word, and sound. The aesthetics of sight and sound come together architecturally in decorative water fountains and in Frank Lloyd Wright's famous house, "Fallingwater."

Water-inspired classic compositions include works such as Debussy's *La Mer (the sea),* Ravel's *Jeux d'eau (Water Games/Fountains),* Mendelssohn's *Calm Sea and Prosperous Voyage* and *Hebrides Overture,* Wagner's *Tristan und Isolde,* and Handel's *Water Music.* Traditional folk music often addresses water-related themes, whether the storytelling vehicle is a sea shanty, minstrel tune, or a ballad.

Journal Prompt

These pages are designed to help you build the knowledge in yourself and your team. Make a note here of the things that children say about puddles.

Which areas of knowledge could be developed with the children you have?

How do the different age groups respond to the experience?

Copy these pages or download a printable version from
www.mindstretchers.academy/series-downloads

Use this page to draw a diagram to help you understand how something is formed (e.g. Raindrops, waterfalls, ripples on a puddle)

List the Lines of Inquiry that children have explored. Dating them will allow you to monitor repeated interests across year groups.

2
Planning Possibilities

The nature pedagogy approach is built on a foundation of co-constructivist thinking, which brings together the intentional adult and the child into a pedagogical dance (*Learning With Nature,* Warden 2015). This means that even when we explore nature-based pedagogies, there are times when the adult leads play and learning and others when the child leads. This is the balance we try to achieve to ensure that the adult has the awareness of the curriculum and milestones that are developmentally appropriate while consulting and empowering children through recording and acting upon their ideas, plans and theories.

The activity of planning should be joyful as it is full of the possibilities of the things to come. When we think about what we can do for children, we are, in essence, planning. When we record this dynamic process in a format that can easily be accessed by other members of the team, it starts to guide group experiences and opportunities. There are a number of things to reflect upon as we explore this playful, inquiry-based approach, such as:

- How do you decide what to do in your program?

- To what extent do you use children's ideas in the program rather than all your own?

- Is there a clear link between what children say, do, make or write and the actions you take in your planning?

⬦ Some children are not always aware of the choices and possibilities they have in the setting. How do you support all children to be aware of the things they could do? How do you start the conversation?

Using Floorbooks® is part of the solution as they are focussed on planning with and for children (*Planning With and For Children,* Warden 2020). There are four strategies that are key to planning in this way:

⬦ The Floorbook®: a large book that is the central hub for working documentation,

⬦ The Talking Tub: a box of provocations created that is linked to Lines of Inquiry,

⬦ The Family Books: individual evidence of the learning that are available to children,

⬦ The Planning Journal: operational planning and observation notes collated by staff linked to the Floorbook®/Family Books.

The difference between a Floorbook® and a large scrapbook is that it is guided by wide Lines of Inquiry, or main ideas, that are being explored by children. With the elements of water, earth, air, and fire all being in the natural world at once, many Lines of Inquiry are the result of changes to these elements. When focussing on the water element through a context such as puddles, we can then explore things like the evaporation of a puddle, frozen and unfrozen water, and changing the speed of water flow from A to B. When we focus on the main idea underneath activities, it allows us to create links between the experiences for children and provide opportunities for deeper conversations.

 ## Line of Inquiry

The myriad of conversations that take place in a group of children all have value and purpose, but sometimes as the educator we can identify an underlying Line of Inquiry. This is a fascination that persists over time and becomes a central idea that is explored in many ways through the duration of the inquiry.

The Line of Inquiry or central idea has some characteristics that support us to understand if we have reached it:

- The central idea is written in one sentence e.g., the movement of water, temporary change (ice and water),

- It expresses concisely an enduring understanding e.g., the inquiry explored a link between mass and movement,

- It is substantial enough to generate in–depth inquiries e.g., movement and characteristics of water is broad enough for depth but not as wide as the whole of movement,

- An effective Line of Inquiry is often concept driven,

- It is relevant, engaging, and significant,

- It allows for action to be taken in a way that makes sense to children.

The Talking Tub

Having tangible objects for children to touch and explore has a direct link to their engagement and vocabulary. Through offering a nature-centered Talking Tub, we can explore curriculum subjects through a context that is exciting and motivational. When the children talk about the objects, the adults record their ideas in the Floorbook® as quotes or through film and audio as a QR code to bring together digital and hard copy documentation.

The materials stay in the Talking Tub and are for use at a gathering time with adults. This means that more fragile elements can be included.

Talking Tubs enhance practice by:

- Making it easier for children to link experiences that take place outside to experiences inside (a puddle outside / water tray inside),

- Developing language through the inclusion of fascinating objects to talk about as a group with an adult,

- Including everyone in the planning process. As children look at images and handle objects they become more aware of the choices they have,

- Stimulating thinking and broadening awareness of the natural world around them.

The table on the next page gives the Lines of Inquiry and suggests materials and objects to collect to deepen the conversations you have with children.

Visual Mind Maps

A visual mind map is used to offer some of the possibilities to children. It is created by the adult who should include the experiences that previous groups of children have shown an interest in.

- The visual mind map is usually created through a material encounter, such as puddles (which I have found to be more meaningful to children),

- Children can draw and add their ideas to the Visual mind map during the session,

- Children decode the map themselves through the images,

- Adults can use photos to embellish the mind map rather than hand drawings,

- A smaller version of the mind map plan is included in the Floorbook® so that more ideas can beadded around it to extend existing Lines of Inquiry.

The adult can of course create a mind map with children. If it is challenging to engage all the children and gather everyone's ideas, using the Talking Tub as the adult can note interest in an object or an image as a sign of preference or motivation.

The separation of the experiences and opportunities is subdivided into curriculum subject areas in another chapter. If you work in an environment that requires planning by defined subject, the Lines of Inquiry would be all academic rather than broader concepts as shared in the example here.

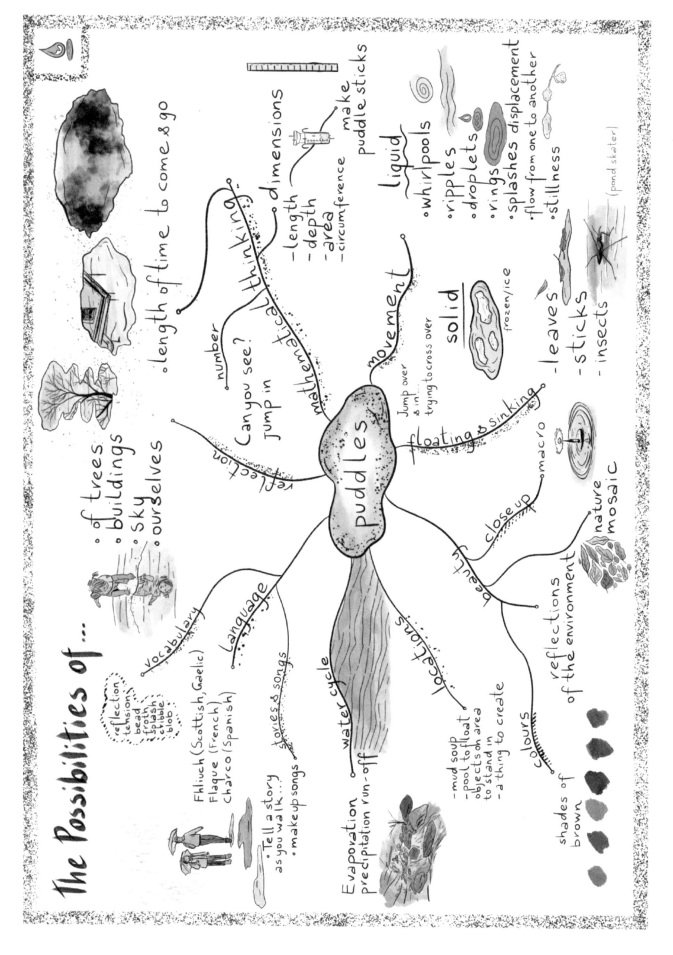

The Possibilities of...

Puddles

- of trees
- buildings
- sky
- ourselves

· length of time to come & go

thinking
- Can you see?
- Jump in

number

mathematical
- dimensions
  - length
  - depth
  - area
  - circumference

make puddle sticks

liquid
- whirlpools
- ripples
- droplets
- rings
- splashes displacement
- flow from one to another
- stillness

(pond skater)

solid
frozen/ice

- leaves
- sticks
- insects

movement
Jump over & in.
trying to cross over

floating & sinking

macro

close up

nature mosaic

beauty

reflections of the environment

reflection

Language

vocabulary
- reflection
- (tension)
- bead
- froth
- splash
- dribble
- blob

Fhliuch (Scottish, Gaelic)
Flaque (French)
charco (Spanish)

- Tell a story as you walk...
- stories & songs
- make up songs

water cycle
Evaporation
precipitation run-off

locations
- mud soup
- pool to float
- objects on area to stand in
- a thing to create

colours

shades of brown

Line of Inquiry	Objects
Properties and use of water	Images of solid (ice), liquid (water) and gas (air). Real examples when you use the Talking Tub. Images of local areas of water such as a puddle, rivers, lakes, and the sea.
Reflections	Photos of reflections in puddles of your environment.
Movement	Images of whirlpools, ripples, rings, droplets, etc.
Floating and sinking	Images of home made boats, leaves floating on puddle, water based insects / water tension. Real materials that could be used to explore the concept, such as a feather, leaf, stone, and mud.
Beauty	Art based imagery of puddles and small areas of water. Creative responses to puddles in charcoal, photography, clay, etc.
Locations for play	Images of diverse children playing such as creating a muddy puddle, floating leaves or flowers on a puddle, or standing in a puddle with boots on.
Water cycle	Images of an overview of the water cycle and specific images of rivers, the sea, puddles, desert, and clouds.
Language development	Words in diverse languages to name and describe puddles to support adult interaction if children cannot yet read. Strong powerful images that evoke language. Real shallow bowl of water like a pretend puddle to explore that can then link to outdoors and real puddles.
Mathematical thinking	Materials such tape measures, rulers/example of a measuring stick, and string for circumference.

Summary Mind Maps - The Learning Journey

The visual mind maps are all around planning for possibilities. The reality is that to be responsive, you may not reach all the ideas, so at the back of the Floorbook® the adult draws a summary mind map (usually without pictures) of what actually happened in the inquiry. This is called the Learning Journey. The summary mind map can then be used to note down the Floorbook® page where the evidence is documented of what happened in your program.

Compiling the Learning Journey as you go through the inquiry gives an overview of curriculum but also grants the flexibility to be more child-centered in your practice.

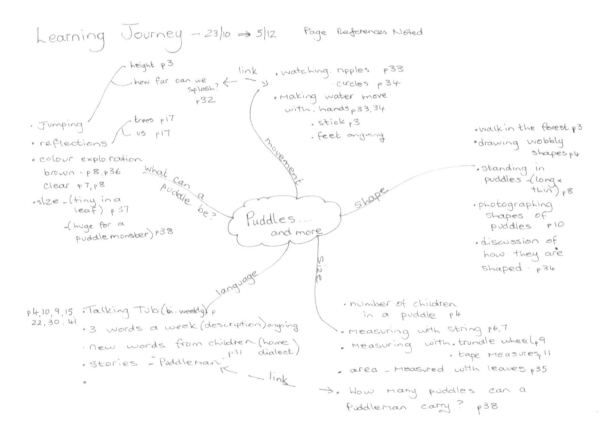

The journal pages in this section are designed for you to note what the children in your space enjoy doing. This ensures that planning is place-based and connects to the culture and community you work in.

These pages are for you to organize the ideas that children share over the years. Use these blank mind map pages to note down children's ideas and theories.

Journal Prompt

How can you use images to make them more accessible?

What big ideas or experiences do children repeatedly enjoy?

Copy these pages or download a printable version from
www.mindstretchers.academy/series-downloads

3
Curricular Links

There are two ways to approach the curriculum: one is through discrete subjects, as can be seen below, while the other is to offer opportunities that are contextual, as shared within the Planning Possibilities chapter.

Each section in this chapter provides the Line of Inquiry and some of the experiential opportunities to explore it. The journal pages are organized into curricular subjects as a guide to your planning.

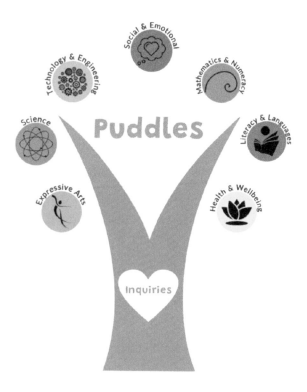

Fascination of Water: Puddles

Area of Inquiry

1. Conceptual knowledge about the creation of puddles (Case Study 2)
2. Observations of evaporation
3. Experimenting with flotation and sinking (Case Study 1)

Area of Inquiry

1. Puddles as a provocation for artistic expression (Case Study 1)
2. Creation of puddle painting

Area of Inquiry

1. Development of technology in rain water use
2. Exploration of water flow

Area of Inquiry

1. Recording mathematical thinking
2. Encourage mathematical concepts such as shape, circumference, area, and depth (Case Study 1)

Area of Inquiry

1. Puddles as a stimulation for different types of writing
2. Talking and listening about a puddle
3. Letter and number formation in a puddle

Area of Inquiry

1. Children's awareness and management of risk (Case Study 3)
2. Active outdoor learning experiences (Case Study 2 and 3)
3. Water as a vital source for well being
4. Atmospheric effect of rain

Area of Inquiry

1. Historical use of water by humans
2. Natural resources in the environment
3. Exploration of the social and emotional link surrounding the weather

Science

Area of Inquiry Concept / Knowledge / Skill	Opportunities of Experiential Learning Experiences
1. Conceptual knowledge about the creation of puddles	
A puddle can be formed by either a depression in the surface or by surface tension.	Within your setting, explore areas where puddles are likely to form and discuss why this might be. Once rain arrives, allow children the time to observe the formation of these puddles.
A puddle can be formed naturally or by children through play.	Around the puddle, discuss how and where the water has come from. Explore natural puddles or plan and design a puddle park by changing the landscape to make depressions, embankments, and canals to see if the rain fills them.
2. Observations of evaporation	
Water in a puddle can evaporate. What causes the puddle to disappear and where does the water go once it has gone?	Chalk out or mark the area of the puddle circumference and depth. Over the session and multiple days, return to observe the change in size and depth of your puddle. Also, discuss where evaporation sits within the water cycle.
Develop knowledge on the erosive influence that water has on natural and manufactured materials through freeze-thaw action and the force of water movement/impact.	Provide opportunities for children to explore and discover your setting and investigate signs of the impact of water erosion on your surrounding environment. Experiment with wood, mud, sand, and metal and observe the erosive influence water has on each–this is best done seasonally to explore temperature as a parameter.

Area of Inquiry Concept / Knowledge / Skill	Opportunities of Experiential Learning Experiences
1.	
2.	

Science

Area of Inquiry Concept / Knowledge / Skill	Opportunities of Experiential Learning Experiences
3. Experimenting with flotation and sinking	
Objects float on water when they displace their own weight.	Allow children to experiment with different materials to investigate their flotation properties. Children will naturally place objects into a puddle and experiment with them. Provide a variety of materials for them to experiment with and discuss with them their theories as to why this occurs.
Water can "hold" particles (suspension).	Create opportunities for children to explore muddy water mixtures. Using clear containers will allow the children to see how the particles settle out when the water is still.

Science

Area of Inquiry Concept / Knowledge / Skill	Opportunities of Experiential Learning Experiences
1.	
2.	

Expressive Arts

Area of Inquiry Concept / Knowledge / Skill	Opportunities of Experiential Learning Experiences
1. Puddles as a provocation for artistic expression	
Puddles have been used by photographers to capture the reflective properties to capture images of the world around them. Music has been used by famous artists such as Gene Kelly in the musical "Singin in the Rain" to express feelings and thoughts whilst dancing through rain and puddles.	Children can be given the opportunity to use cameras to capture the reflections that are found within puddles. Allow children the opportunity to dance and express themselves whilst out playing in puddles. A video camera can record this motion and be set to music later–perhaps recorded by the children. Children could also be supported to use the experience of puddles for anecdotal writing, such as poetry about their experiences of puddles.
2. Creation of puddle painting	
The water from puddles can be combined with plant matter, soil, and berries to create natural paints, or to simply change the hue of the puddle.	Simply using the puddle as paint, have children use a brush, stick, or finger to create works of art on the ground or walls. These can be photographed and reflected on, providing a rich stimulation for language. This can be extended through making earth colored paints. Soil varies so much in color from one garden to the next. The children can bring in their soil and create a varied pallet of mud paint.

Area of Inquiry Concept / Knowledge / Skill	Opportunities of Experiential Learning Experiences
1.	
2	

Area of Inquiry Concept / Knowledge / Skill	Opportunities of Experiential Learning Experiences
1. Development of technology in rain water use	
The development of technology in harnessing rainwater provides the opportunity to learn about industry, machinery, and production methods.	Children can be given the opportunity to research the ways that people have used machines and resources to manipulate rainwater. Small rates of production using a small water mill can be compared to the mass production in industry. A water wheel can be created by children. Please refer to the adult skill chapter for more information.
2. Exploration of water flow	
Water has been a part of the cultural heritage of people around the world. This opportunity can focus on the engineering challenges of construction but also lead into historical conversations about the use of water.	Provide a variety of drain pipes, gutters, and flexible tubing to create a canal system with changes of angles and levels. The more complex the materials, the richer the language and learning will be. It is useful to have objects to put into the channels to test the flow.

Dr. Claire Warden

Technology & Engineering

Area of Inquiry Concept / Knowledge / Skill	Opportunities of Experiential Learning Experiences
1.	
2.	

Area of Inquiry Concept / Knowledge / Skill	Opportunities of Experiential Learning Experiences
1. Recording mathematical thinking	
The use of rain gauges between your setting and home can be used to help motivate children to engage with math.	Create rain gauges so that the children can record precipitation within the setting, compare and contrast over a period of time, and set up as a home link to compare rainfall from setting to home.
2. Encourage mathematical concepts such as shape, circumference, area and depth	
Explore using a range of standard measuring equipment (e.g. tape measures) and non-standard measuring equipment (e.g. stick, hand, leaf).	Experiment with different measuring tools to record the depth of a puddle. Outline the puddle using chalk to measure its shape and circumference, using this chalk as a measurement on how quickly evaporation occurs. While counting out or using a stop watch to record time trials, children and adults walk around the puddle to see how long it takes to do a lap around each puddle. Estimate how many buckets it takes to fill a puddle, then test out the children's estimation. Explore the area using leaves or other material to cover the surface.

Area of Inquiry Concept / Knowledge / Skill	Opportunities of Experiential Learning Experiences
1.	
2.	

Area of Inquiry Concept / Knowledge / Skill	Opportunities of Experiential Learning Experiences
1. Puddles as a stimulation for different types of writing	
Children may choose to write while outside (waterproof notepads and pens) or reflect upon experience back in setting.	Using puddles as stimulation, promote children to use descriptive language or write poetry about their sensorial experiences with it. The fact that children can do so many things with water means that it is a perfect object for them to use as a focus for discussion and writing.
2. Talking and listening about a puddle	
Explore feelings, factual information, and even the sound effects associated with a puddle.	The experience of being around a puddle can create a calming atmosphere that supports children to take part in a range of speaking and listening activities. They can explore their reflections as they talk.
3. Letter and number formation in a puddle	
Create a mark making tool or use natural materials to make a writing surface to explore their effects in and on puddles.	Use the flat water surface as a magic writing board. Use a long stick as the writing tool. Draw letters and numbers on some leaves, put them into the puddles, and float them to form words or sums.

Area of Inquiry Concept / Knowledge / Skill	Opportunities of Experiential Learning Experiences
1.	
2.	

Health & Wellbeing	Area of Inquiry Concept / Knowledge / Skill	Opportunities of Experiential Learning Experiences
1. Children's awareness and management of risk		
	Children are able to self-risk assess, and the more we can trust them to make decisions and provide supportive environments for them to do so, the more they will thrive.	Children can be supported to create their own Benefit Risk Assessment about engaging with puddles. This will encourage them to make decisions about how to look after themselves and others. The risk assessment can be written down by children or recorded from their own words by an adult.
2. Active outdoor learning experiences		
	Children develop fine and gross motor skills moving around, over, and through puddles and outdoor spaces in their search for puddles.	Children can be encouraged to explore the outdoor area and look for puddles or signs of puddles on dry days. If there are no signs of puddles within the setting, they could be given the task of searching for puddles in their own home environment or local park and finding out why the puddle has formed there.
3. Water as a vital source for well being		
	Explore thirst and how much water we consume in a day. Do we know if we have drank enough to stay healthy?	Have discussions on the vital need for us to have water and what the consequences are for not having enough water. Encourage children to regulate their water intake, especially on warmer days. Provide access to water and allow the children to access it when they require it to promote independence. However, be mindful of the children and monitor them from a distance when they do access water.
4. Atmospheric effect of rain		
	Children enjoy the sight, sound, touch, smell, and even taste of rain.	Organize a reflective discussion outside that is sheltered from the rain. The soothing sound of the rain on the roof and all around can help children focus on the discussion of rain and create a calming atmosphere. This can be a perfect opportunity to talk about feelings and emotions to do with ourselves and each other.

Health & Wellbeing

Area of Inquiry Concept / Knowledge / Skill	Opportunities of Experiential Learning Experiences
1.	
2.	

Social & Emotional

Area of Inquiry Concept / Knowledge / Skill	Opportunities of Experiential Learning Experiences
1. Historical use of water by humans	
Water is required by all people on the earth to survive. However, how it is used other than being a basic requirement varies from one culture to another.	Have the children do research using the internet to find out how water is used by different people around the world. For example, a tip tap used in Africa can be created by the children.
2. Natural resources in the environment	
Rainwater can be a sustainable energy source if it is used sensibly and we look after it.	Research with the children why recycling rainwater in sensible quantities can make it a sustainable resource. Create mini or large water butts and monitor the water saved.
3. Weather: the social and emotional link	
	Discuss how different weather conditions make us feel and what we do in different weather conditions. Consider starting to record the daily weather conditions and link that data with activities and emotions.

Area of Inquiry Concept / Knowledge / Skill	Opportunities of Experiential Learning Experiences
1.	
2.	

4
Daily Planning

Planning needs to be responsive as it is adapted to the weather, group dynamic of the children, unexpected opportunities, and staffing. Although there is always some intent in the experiences and opportunities we engage with, the exact outcome will be different for every child. It is this child centered nature of education that makes it so effective. As the experiences have some planning behind them, it cannot be described as pure play, which by its very nature is spontaneous and unplanned.

However, they are what you would call open-ended, meaning a provocation is offered and the children respond by playing with materials such as puddles. The adults may place the mathematical equipment near the puddle because they know children have been theorizing on how to measure all the puddles in the yard. This action is a provocation and is less structured than an invitation where the adult may say "Could you measure puddles today?" The most adult direct approach would be to say, "Now that we are measuring puddles, here is a tape measure, a worksheet, and two puddles for you to observe and make drawings of." This interaction is seen as adult directed as children have no choice about the time, the resources, or what they may do.

The planning journal is the place where the operational notes are recorded for everyone to access. There are elements that are included to link to the inquiry-based approach in the Floorbooks®.

Line of Inquiry

As explained in the planning possibilities chapter, if the whole team is aware of some underlying fascinations of the children, their interactions with the children can help them explore their inquiries further.

 Possible Line of Development (P.L.O.D)

Linked to the content of the Floorbook®, Possible Lines of Development are written like a next step. If we wrote that the next step was to "find a puddle", it doesn't convey why the experience or opportunity is taking place. It could be that it links to an outcome in the curriculum or a broader concept. So, it could be:

- "Find a puddle to explore the ups and downs of the site," or

- "Go on a puddle hunt to see our faces in the water."

The documentation of the playful experiences would then go back into the Floorbook® through the photos and words you wrote down.

 Focus

Planning journals are designed to improve practice and include supporting adult interactions. Writing down a specific thing to focus on supports adults to have a purpose within the experience alongside their general support and care of children. If the P.L.O.D. is "Go on a puddle hunt to see our faces in the water," what will the adult be doing? Will the adult be consciously using descriptive words, taking time to get ready into wet weather gear, encouraging children to explore, and/or talking about the features of a face?

Link

When adults and children make links between different areas of learning or links between an experience at home and in the setting, it helps them learn.

An example might be that a child has been sharing how they jump in puddles in the park. We note that on the planning journal and the initial of the child, so any member of the team can make the links in our conversation. Nature-based experiences do have opportunities for very complex ideas and progression in learning, but the learning is not written on the side of a resource box. The adult has to be aware of the possibilities across the locations that a child encounters, hence the reason for these books.

Focussing on inside, outside, and beyond is written about elsewhere (*Learning With Nature,* Warden 2015), but let us just consider how the experience of looking in a puddle is encountered differently across three locations and how we can be mindful of this when we make links in our planning.

Inside Shelters, Buildings	Outside Outdoor Areas	Beyond Home Garden, Park, Wilder Areas, Community
● Still, shallow bowls of water to look in ● Artificial light ● Table or floor ● Small group	● Puddle areas created with plastic sheet or naturally formed surfaces ● Daylight ● Muddy, wet ground ● Flexible group	● Puddles found with family ● Hard ground like a path ● Individual or siblings ● Wilder spaces could be with early years group

Engage

The younger the child, the more intuitive and responsive the adult needs to be as the child responds to the world around them. All children deserve to be with adults who consider how they will offer an experience or an opportunity. When we offer a play provocation, we can do it beautifully and carefully or not. Being nature-based does not equate to not being careful and thoughtful about what we do and how we create our environments. Children learn from observing adults, and they will take note of the care you take of the natural world and the resources it shares with us. In this section of the daily planning, we note as a team that we will engage the children. An example might be "Gather under the storytelling tree with the calling song. Tell the story of the Puddle Jumper to initiate a conversation about catching a puddle. Check the availability of resources such as cotton string, markers, and wood whittling tools in case they want to make puddle measurers."

The process of reflection is ongoing. Adults do it all the time, and when working in a nature-based environment, they do it more. Many team members have individual reflective journals that they complete as part of their continual professional development. This section is different to those as it is targeted towards quality improvement as a team as we build rich, stimulating environments for playful inquiries.

The planning cycle includes a process of reviewing what happened so that we continually learn. After the intentional experiences are finished, the planning sheet asks you to consider three things before you consider what to do next.

 Investigate

We always need to be open to the idea that children will bring something new to the experience. How did the children respond? What do they want to learn more about?

 Documentation

Documentation can be done through what children do, say, make and write. As noted in the planning possibilities chapter, think about who you are documenting for.

Make observation notes in this section of what children did. Were there new words? A moment of wonder? Make a note of where the images taken today should go. Is there an individual learning story or perhaps images taken for the Floorbook®?

 Reflect

Planning is about improving the experiences and opportunities you offer at set points in the day and being organized to respond to children and their pure play through continuous provision. Not every day is perfect, and sometimes it is good to take the time to record if there were challenges about the opportunities you offered.

 P.L.O.D.s

The next group of P.L.O.D.s can be taken directly from the Floorbook®, or they may just come from the unplanned conversations and observations. Writing those down in your daily planning means that the planning coordinator can read the sheets and take children's ideas forward.

The planning cycle, or rather planning spiral, never really ends as hours flow into days, and weeks into months. The Floorbook® and Talking Tub are used throughout inquiries whether they are nature based or not, and the detail of exactly what takes place is written down in the daily planning.

Journal Prompt

These pages are for the operational notes on what will happen every day in your program. They link to the Lines of Inquiry (L.O.I.) and the Possible Lines of Development (P.L.O.D.) that you have gathered from the Floorbook® and general observations of the children.

WEEKLY OVERVIEW

MONDAY	TUESDAY	WEDNESDAY

THURSDAY	FRIDAY	NOTES

REMINDERS

◆ _____   ◆ _____

◆ _____   ◆ _____

◆ _____   ◆ _____

Line of Inquiry -

What is the broad underlying main idea in this experience?

P.L.O.D. -

What are you planning to do?

Focus -

What is the intentional focus of the planned experiences? It could be an area of curriculum such as numbers to 10, the use of vocabulary, engagement of key children, muscle control, and joy.

Link -

How are you relating this to children's previous learning?

Engage -

How will you engage children? What resources do you need to get ready? Where will you offer the provocation/invitation?

After the experience fill these areas in.

? **Investigate -**
How did the children respond? What do they want to learn more about?

Documentation -

What did children actually do, say, make, and write? Is it going in the Floorbook®, individual portfolios, or on display?

Reflect -

How did it go for you and the children? What changes would you make if you did it again?

Next P.L.O.D. -

What is the next step in the learning journey for these children?

Use this page to reflect on the impact of your planning on the quality of experience that children have.

Things to keep the same.

Things to change.

NOTES:

5
Case Studies with Analysis and Possible Lines of Development

As part of this philosophy, we encourage children to be involved in documentation. The images in this chapter include those taken by both practitioners and children.

These images would be printed out and used within the Floorbook®. In the morning of each day, children are encouraged to cut out and stick in the photographs they think are most important. On occasions where the learning is significant, the entire case study is shared in the Family Book as evidence of individual engagement.

Case Study 1: The REAL Potential of a Puddle!

On the rainiest day of the year, two 4 year old boys decided to explore some puddles. This is their story…

In a part of our garden, there are a whole series of puddles left over from various digging experiments of the past. Two boys were drawn to this area, and they were off to "test the puddles."

To begin with, the boys were a little cautious, so they carried out mini-risk/wellie (rubber rain boots) depth assessments. They would enter slowly from the side and move across the puddle to check the depth right into the middle. Once they were sure that the puddle was not too deep, they would jump in.

We started to talk about how deep the puddles were:

"It's okay, none of these go over your wellies."

Adult:
"How do we know how deep it is?"

"We could check it with a stick!"

Then, one of the boys got a very short stick, and it went in up to his hand. *"This stick's too small, I need a bigger one." "Wow! That's pretty deep–nearly half the stick."*

"I know, I'm 'gonna' test it with me.
Yep, it's not over my
wellies–it's not that deep."

The boys then moved around the puddles, exploring depths and testing them with sticks and other items. One of the boys then noticed that some of the things were floating in the water and started to discuss this with his friend.

"Look! Our measuring stick floats, and those leaves."

"But that one is sinking."

"It's 'cause you splashed it with water and it got heavy."

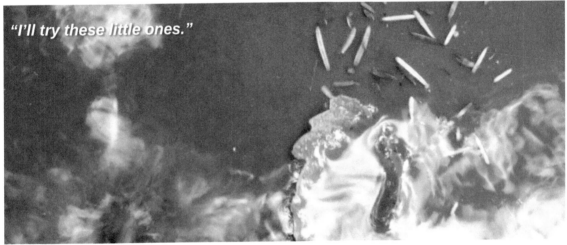

The boys then fished around using their measuring stick, and, eventually, they somehow found it and dragged it to the side.

"There it is, let's try again."

"What about this? This will float."

They then tried a wood "cookie" that was the same size as the stone but made of wood. The boys then moved out of the woodland cover into the garden and discovered two things about the next puddle.

"Look, I can see me! And there are bubbles. Where are the bubbles from?" The boys moved to see their reflection move and kept on staring at the bubbles. *"The rain is splashing and it turns into a bubble, look, and now it's gone!"*

"It only lasts a minute–why is that?"

"It's not washing up liquid, it's just natural in there."

The boys then checked to see if the other puddles had bubbles and discovered the only puddles that had bubbles were those in the garden and not those under the trees. They thought it could be due to the size, so they measured a few puddles.

"No, these are the same as over there."

Adult:
"Is there anything above us here in the garden compared to over there in the woods?"

"There is just sky here, there are trees there."

Adult:
"So do you think that makes a difference to how the raindrop falls in the puddle?"

"I don't know... "

The boys went off to explore more about puddles and what they could put in them.

The next day we reflected upon what we had learned about puddles in the camp journal and talked more about these strange bubbles. We decided to watch the puddles on a different day, when it wasn't raining quite so hard, to see what happened and if the bubbles were there.

Analysis of Learning

The boys explored many aspects of puddles: their shape, size and depth (mathematics), reflections, floating/sinking, and bubble formation (science). They spent a considerable period of time exploring these aspects and talking with each other regarding their theories and ideas. Finding the bubbles was the only thing that confused the boys, and on that day, we didn't push the discussion as this would be a subject to explore further on other rainy days.

P.L.O.D.s

1. Explore puddles on different days to see if bubbles form, where bubbles form the most, and formulate a theory as to why they form. Children may wish to create their own puddles and try to make their own bubbles by dropping dropping objects into the water, stirring to see the link between air, gravity, and water.

2. Watch puddles over a day or several days to explore how they change and how they are linked to weather conditions, as well as other factors. This could be done physically with chalk, flour, or string for marking boundaries, or photographically.

3. Experiment further with floating and sinking by using different objects and different locations. Evidence could be collected through photography or video and reflected upon at a later date.

Case Study 2: Linking Puddles Learning Story

Two boys, one aged 5 and one aged 4, decided that they wanted to make one huge puddle and would do this by cutting channels, linking them with a spade. One of the children had had this interest while at nursery several years before.

Adult:
"What are you doing boys?"

"The puddles are racing, we are joining them up."

The boys then continued their discussions of where to dig to link all the puddles together. Laurie was sensibly selecting areas with the shortest distance between puddles (he knows what hard work digging is!). As he dug out the channel, the water started to flow and run from one to the other.

"This one is winning, it's going faster!" said the younger boy.

The older boy dug faster, deeper, and wider to speed up the process. As the water balanced out, the flow slowed and the older boy observed:

"Look, look! This one isn't as deep as before, some water must have gone in there."

Adult:
"What's your plan?"

The oldest child responded:

"To join them all up and make one big puddle."

The boys continued to create channels until all the puddles were linked.

While still digging to join the puddles, the boys started to discuss and explore the stones.

Adult:
"It's a bit like gold panning! What do you think you will find?"

The older boy, who had seen gold panning on the television, started to swirl his spade and keep it flat in an attempt to sift out the stones from the mud. He then spotted two different stones.

Adult:
"Ooh! That one is quartz, bright white–look."

Older boy:
"I don't like that one, I like this stone, see how smooth and round it is."

Adult:
"Do you think it got smoothed by the water?"

Older boy:
"No, it's just like that–I'm 'gonna' take it home."

The boys continued to pan and explore the puddles and, to my knowledge, they found no gold!

Analysis of Learning

The boys were revisiting learning that they had undertaken in the past, building on their understanding of the properties of water and their skills of digging. The boys were highly focused and spent over an hour, with much of it independent of an adult selecting where to dig and creating their "big puddle." The children learnt a great deal about flow, gravity, and the properties of water. They developed their skills in using the spade, both to dig and "pan for gold." Interest moved into the properties of soil and types of stones. This experience demonstrated excellent co-operative learning between a mixed age group, fantasy play of racing puddles, mathematics, and science.

P.L.O.D.s

1. Explore the properties of water further; introduce a plum line and level to explore the role of gradient in water flow. A trip can be taken to a stream, or further water runways can be developed through digging them out or using pipes and gutters.

2. Investigate stones, what stones we find where, their texture, color, and so on. A Talking Tub could be constructed in conjunction with a 3D mind map to link to the stones.

3. Investigate the properties of soil and soil type. Filters can be created to separate the soil, or a comparison between the soil in the garden, natural river clay and commercial clays (different craft clay) can be undertaken to explore the differences and what we can do with them.

4. Develop the idea of gold panning and allow the children to set up role-play situations or treasurehunts. They may choose to "plant" treasure in the soil for others to find/pan.

Case Study 3: A Very Rainy Day... and Bridges

This was a typical Scottish summer's day. Where the heavens opened, two of the younger boys from camp (both aged 4) were enjoying the huge puddle that was forming outside the Kinder Kitchen. They paced through it, skipped through it, ran through it, and jumped in and out of it. They then started to realize that when their parents came to pick them up, how would they get into the camp without getting their feet wet?

"We should make a bridge, then everyone can get in without getting wet feet."

"Where should we put it?" "Here."

"It wobbles here, move it around." "We need a 'measurer' to see if it is long enough."

"It's too short!"

"We can move it and add up the length, it's OK, it's long enough–we can jump."

They then moved down to the bottom area near the tool working zone.

"We need another bridge–here too."

"Bricks... we can use them."

"It's too long a step, we need to move it closer. Does it wobble?"

"Move the stones underneath."

"OK, it's safe, step over."

"We need a bridge on top to go under it too. Kate hold that!"

Once these bridges were complete, the boys went off to explore puddles in other parts of the garden.

Later on that day, the same two boys were creating their own role-play game linked to Peter Pan in the sand pit (which at Auchlone is shaped like a boat, as voted for by the children).

They again returned to the theme of water and bridges:

"We need a bridge... walk the plank".
"We need a bridge to get on and off the boat over the water."

The boy's collected the "bridge" they had made earlier on, over by the Kinder Kitchen.

"This is a pirate ship, we are Peter Pans, and this is our bridge. OK, it's wobbly, we need to move it."

The boys moved the plank around the various positions, with an adult watching from a safe distance to ensure they were remembering how to stay safe.

"I will test it... hold my hand Kate, it's a little slippery."

Adult:
"Why?"

"It's raining–we must be careful.
We need to stop it wobbling.
I will get a log."

The boys went to get a log.

"It's too short!"

"We need more. There's a gap–fill it."

The boys then made several round trips to collect the large heavy logs from the other side of the garden. As they returned, they moved the logs around under the plank to make sure they were adjusted by height, digging them in where they needed to, and constantly reminding each other to "watch your fingers," "is it wobbly?" and "it's still slippery–stay safe".

Finally, they were happy with the stability, angle, and location of their bridge, and this became their access route to their ship. Other children came to join in, and the two boys showed them how to walk on the "slippery bridge" safely.

The following day, one of the boys helped write up the learning that took place in our camp journal. He stuck in the photographs, reflecting on the learning and experience of the previous day. These ideas were transcribed by a member of staff in his own words.

Analysis of Learning

During this case study, the primary focus of the children was to explore access routes and different methods of crossing space. During the course of this experience, the children were constantly assessing the hazards and associated risks of the activity, formulating their own risk assessments. The children also worked cooperatively to handle and move large planks and heavy logs into the correct location. These experiences led to some fantastic contextual learning about height, length, and depth, as well as the effects of water on wood, stone and sand.

P.L.O.D.s

1. Film videos or create photographic sequential storyboards of the children's risk–assessing learning activity. These can be shown to parents, new children, or be used to remind children of the risk assessments they have undertaken and how to safely undertake learning activities and experiences.

2. Explore bridges and crossing methods that are familiar to children, such as local sites and national landmarks. Look at their different construction methods and perhaps replicate styles (in model or large scale form) to explore why certain types of crossings are used in different locations. This is closely linked with the schemas of boundary and connection.

3. Undertake a planning session for real activity with the children, exploring the landscape of your site, flood zone, and streams, as well as seeing if bridges or crossing methods should be put in place. Implement decisions made through consultation.

These pages are designed for you to notice and take notes about the kinds of things that your children find fascinating.

Journal Prompt

How do you document the play and learning that takes place inside and outside?

Journal Prompt

How can you share these amazing moments with families?

Journal Prompt

Where and how do you encourage children to look back at all their adventures?

6
Developing Skills

I n your role as the nature pedagogue it is important to develop yourself as a resource. This will involve you learning new skills, understanding concepts and increasing your knowledge base of the natural world. Here are a few examples from both children and adults as they designed and developed new skills linked to the fascination of puddles. The journal pages encourage you to select four new skills that you wish to develop.

1. Puddle Catcher
(by Steven, 33 years old)

The term puddle catcher was given to the large black builder's tray that is at the center. The children use it to "puddle catch" more often than they do for mud play due to large areas of the forest we work in that are mud pits.

1. If you do not have areas outside where puddles form naturally, you can set up the puddle catcher in your outdoor space.
2. Set out containers for the children to fill up. These can be buckets, cups, or bottles. The children fill up and then transport the water until they are happy with the level of water in the puddle.
3. The problem solving experiences to get the water from the tap to the puddle can be extended through the provision of guttering and rods to make a frame to hold up the guttering. Extend this experience by ensuring that the bamboo guttering comes in a variety of diameters and, therefore, profiles.

4. Provide loose materials for children to place in the puddle or ask them to go out and forage for materials in and around your setting.

5. Be mindful as they explore to pick up any fascinations that could be taken forward.

2. Water Mill

(by Archie, 8 years old)

1. Collect some wood for the paddles.
2. You will need sticks to hold it together.
3. Find nails and some twine to fix the paddles in place.
4. Measure along the wood for how long you need the paddles to be. If it's too long, the paddle will get stuck, and if it's too short, the water won't reach it.
5. Once you are happy with the length of the paddle, you need to saw the wood to its size. You need to get a saw and a glove. The glove goes on your hand before you start and it goes on the hand that you're not holding the saw with.
6. Hammer your nails into the wood, and you can use twine as well to secure it if you need to.
7. Once you are finished and it's OK, go and test it out. You might need to adjust the paddles.
8. When it is working, put two sticks into the ground and place the wheel in between them. The water should push it round and round.

3. Condensation Traps

(by Claire Warden)

Create a puddle from "thin air" by creating a condensation trap.

1. Dig out a wide cone shaped hole in some damp earth.
2. Place a puddle catcher (container) in the base of the cone.
3. Suspend a plastic sheet over the whole cone area.
4. Place a stone on the plastic sheet over the container to create a drip point.
5. Leave overnight or for 24 hours so that the water evaporating from the vegetation and earth is caught on the underside of the plastic.
6. The water will dribble down the sheet and drip into the container to create a drinkable puddle!

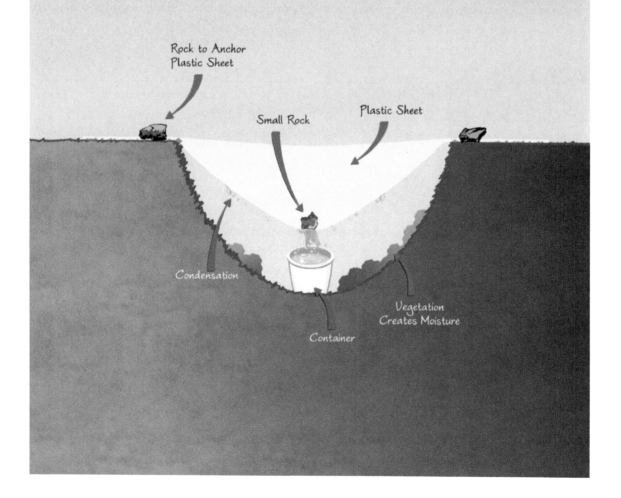

Journal Prompt

Collect resources for new skills that could link to this fascination.

> **Skill 1:** (e.g. Puddle Catcher)

Make a list below of supporting materials for developing this skill.
(Books, Websites, YouTube videos, Podcasts etc.)

- _____

- _____

- _____

- _____

- _____

- _____

- _____

- _____

- _____

- _____

- _____

- _____

- _____

Skill 2: (e.g. Watermill)

Make a list below of supporting materials for developing this skill.
(Books, Websites, YouTube videos, Podcasts etc.)

- _____
- _____
- _____
- _____
- _____
- _____
- _____
- _____
- _____
- _____
- _____

Copy these pages or download a printable version from
www.mindstretchers.academy/series-downloads

Journal Prompt

Skill 3: (e.g. Condensation Trap)

Make a list below of supporting materials for developing this skill.
(Books, Websites, YouTube videos, Podcasts etc.)

Journal Prompt

Skill 4:

Make a list below of supporting materials for developing this skill.
(Books, Websites, YouTube videos, Podcasts etc.)

- _____
- _____
- _____
- _____
- _____
- _____
- _____
- _____
- _____
- _____
- _____

7

Benefit Risk Assessment

The risk management process needs to balance the benefits of experience with any unseen threats that the child and adults may not be aware of. These threats are presented in the form of hazards and can be part of physical, intellectual, social, and emotional risk taking. We as adults often focus on physical hazards because they are easier to observe, but the impact of emotional harm and lack of intellectual stimulation may also have a great impact over a lifetime.

Benefit Risk Management

Undertake a Benefit Risk Assessment (BRA) for the site and all the activities you plan to undertake well before the experience so that you are familiar and aware of the spaces you work in and what the experience or activity entails.

Site Risk Assessment

Map the site to show emergency access in case of emergency and key features of the landscape to ensure that you know where the hazards may be on the site.

Activity Risk Assessment

The form here shows in detail some of the aspects that could cause harm. They could seem extreme for exploring puddles, but one of the important aspects of this work is that safety as a broad concept needs to be in the minds of everyone involved. This is not about removing risk, as we need that to learn, but minimizing the hazards that may be unseen and can cause harm. Risk assessments therefore need to be accessible and read by the whole team

Dynamic Risk Management

The weather, animal life, and mood of the children, as well as the skill and number of adults you are working with, all play a part in the experience. There needs to be a section on any risk assessment for adaptation to the unforeseen circumstances.

Child Voice

Children are the stakeholders in the situation, so their awareness, knowledge, and understanding of hazards should be included as a separate sheet. The Floobook and Talking Tub is very effective at allowing children time to understand materials and objects that, if used inappropriately, could cause harm.

Undertake a benefit risk assessment as part of the process of getting ready. Ask both adults and children the following 3 questions:

- What is good about this activity? (Benefits)

- What do we need to be careful of? (Hazards and associated Risks)

- How do we stay safe? (Precautions)

Example of Site Risk Assessment

Use an existing map of the area that shows all the details or draw your own. Consider road access, habitat areas for animals, vegetation type, steep slopes and cliffs, bodies of water (such as rivers or lakes), and mobile reception. Mark the areas that you will visit and use "What Three Words" (W3W) to find the location reference.

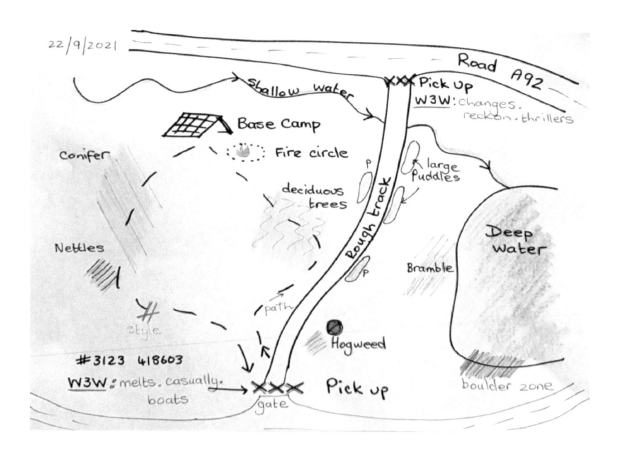

Activity Risk Assessment Example

Benefit-Risk Assessment	**Water Based Activities**
Assessment date: 11/23/21	Date for review: 02/19/22
Assessment undertaken by: GR	Staff member
Approved by: BN	Senior staff member
Local site considerations/amendments:	Unstable tree branches, low level branches, overhang area of trees. Uneven ground conditions or obstacles on the ground. Weather effects on the ground, seating areas and other surfaces. Gradients of slope. Staff/parents/guardian and children
Benefits of activity:	◆ Build independence and develop trust ◆ Group co-operation ◆ Opportunity for participants to self-risk assess. ◆ Build self-confidence ◆ Group awareness ◆ Aesthetics/spirituality/atmosphere ◆ Understanding puddles and water cycles

Fascination of Water: Puddles

Hazard	Level of Risk	Precaution	Assessed Risk Level
Drowning	Medium	● Adults are first aid trained and aware of appropriate CPR	Low
Hypothermia	Medium	● Appropriately dressed in waterproof clothing and protective footwear ● Children's clothing may become soaked through, therefore, an awareness of the signs and symptoms of hypothermia must be known by all staff ● Spare clothing available to change children out of wet gear and into dry ● Access to a warm drink for the child to sip on ● Slowly reheating a child if they become hypothermic ● Warm and dry area to visit if required	Low

Hazard	Level of Risk	Precaution	Assessed Risk Level
Medical conditions	Medium	● Allergies and medical conditions/requirements are checked prior to activity	Variable
Cuts or injuries from puddle exploration	Medium	● Cuts are washed and treated immediately and first aid requirements dealt with appropriately	Low
Environmental impact	Medium/High	● Monitor the environmental impact upon area and desist use if causing severe damage to soil/root structures etc. ● Assess if puddle source is a spring or a depression in the ground	Low
Health hazards	Medium/High	● Contact with micro-organism ● Stagnant water to be checked for signs of pollutant or life	Low

Activity Risk Assessment Template

Benefit-Risk Assessment	Activity
Assessment date:	Date for review:
Assessment undertaken by:	
Approved by:	
Local site considerations/amendments:	
Benefits of activity:	

Hazard	Level of Risk	Precaution	Assessed Risk Level

Copy these pages or download a printable version from https://mindstretchers.academy/series-downloads

Example of a Dynamic Risk Assessment

Benefit Risk Assessment	Water Based Activities
Assessment date: 01/23	Date for review:
Assessment undertaken by: M. Morrow	Staff member
Approved by: C.H. Warden	Senior staff member
Local site considerations/amendments:	Wet, warm rain. Group of 10 children aged 2 years old with 2 adults. In the open play area at the nursery.
Benefits of activity:	◦ Joy ◦ Exploration of displacement and its influence on a material ◦ Empowerment ◦ Social interaction

Hazard	Level of Risk	Precaution	Revised Risk Level
Emotionally upset	Medium	◈ Increase ratio of staff to children today to support the less confident children to play in the puddle ◈ Gradual introduction of the experience to help children choose to engage and take the risk to discover the unknown	Low
Feeling cold (perceived risk)	Medium	◈ Children have puddle suits over their boots ◈ Change of clothes in the cabin ◈ Active play followed by change process in response to their level of self regulation and resilience	Low

Dynamic Risk Management Template

Our role as adults is to be risk aware. These pages are designed to be used to collate your own adjustments to the risk assessments shared. This makes them specific to your space, the weather, the children and the skill of the adults. There should be activity (shared in this chapter), site plans and assessments of the hazards, and dynamic risk management in place.

Benefit-Risk Assessment	Water Based Activities
Assessment date:	Date for review:
Assessment undertaken by:	
Approved by:	
Local site considerations/amendments:	
Benefits of activity:	

Hazard	Level of risk	Precaution	Assessed risk level

Copy these pages or download a printable version from https://mindstretchers.academy/series-downloads

Documenting the Child's Voice in Risk Management

It is very important to involve the stakeholder in risk management. In this case, that is the child. Use the Talking Tub to have the conversations well before you introduce any experiences linked to the use of tools. Noting down what they say, and think is part of the adult assessment, but it is recorded into the group Floorbook® so that you can all revisit it. It allows us to consider the procedures we put in place across different groups of children according to the experience rather than only their age. Understanding and embracing a fascination is at the heart of an emergent curriculum and allows us to be responsive to their inquiry. Our duty of care means that we need to be aware of the implications of children's ideas and be able to risk assess any situation. Sometimes we need to negotiate or put a firm behavioral boundary in place if that opportunity can continue.

Activity Child Voice Template

Use this page to gather children's ideas about how to keep themselves safe. Write on the Lines of Inquiry and issues that you feel could be discussed. Some suggestions would be sticks, deep water, strangers, high winds, fire and use of tools.

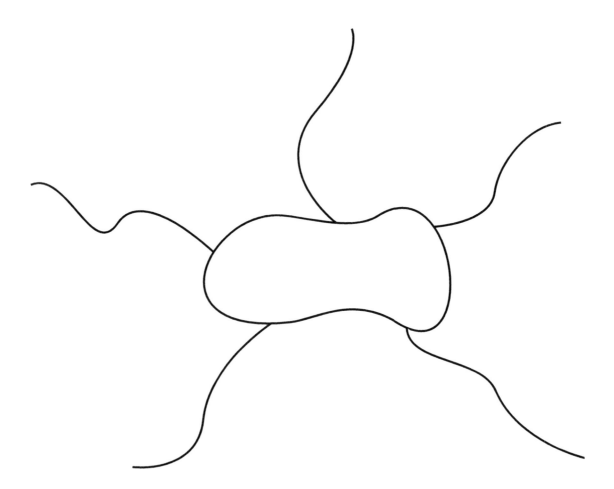

What behaviors from children might affect the activity? Consider how the team will ensure that children have clear boundaries of behavior if you leave the main fenced site.

Journal Prompt

What weather systems do you have in the space that you work? How will these affect the activity? For example, high winds make forests more hazardous due to falling branches.

Consider the adult challenges. How does energy level, clothing, mood, and food affect both adults and children, especially on days when the weather is more challenging?

What shelter structures, equipment, and training do the adults in the team need to help them feel more positive about being out in the rain and playing in puddles?

Summary

The journey to see the potential of a puddle has now hopefully begun. The next time it rains or the water overflows, the reader, hopefully, will see it as a moment of such opportunity for learning that he or she will not be able to resist. The nature of learning is that it happens for children when they are afforded the opportunity to engage in an environment that respects their motivation. Children have many childhood rights, and one of them has to be the joy of jumping in a puddle. Having said that, adults who work with children should have playfulness in their hearts so that they can hold an understanding of the attraction.

This book has been created to support adults to see the benefits of working with the natural elements as a way of teaching and learning. The inclusion of curriculum concepts and skills lead to longer term developments in attitude that stay with the learner throughout their lives. We need to be able to identify and document learning outside to reinforce links across the three learning environments of inside, outside and beyond, if we are to support children, families and educational groups to "be" outside in nature.

If you have found this book useful, then you may want to deepen your understanding of the concepts mentioned by taking courses from the Mindstretchers Academy. Please visit our website for more details.

With kind regards,

Claire

www.mindstretchers.academy

About the Author

D r. Claire Warden is an international education consultant, researcher, advisor, and author. She is the founder of the multiple award winning Auchlone Nature Kindergarten and Mindstretchers Academy which are both based In Scotland, U.K.

Dr. Claire Warden is an educational consultant who has developed her approach to Nature Pedagogy and experiential learning through working in a variety of settings, including her own multi award-winning Auchlone Nature Kindergarten, advisory work, and lecturing in further education. Claire is currently based in Scotland, but she frequently travels to Australia, the United States, and elsewhere. Her unique contribution to the field of education has been recognized through many awards, and she holds her Doctorate in the "Creation and theorisation of Nature Pedagogy".

Claire is an author of over 20 books relating to early years methodology. Claire's book, *Learning with Nature – Embedding Outdoor Practice*, was well received and has gained a place as required reading on many academic education courses. In her book *Nature Kindergartens and Forest Schools*, Claire explores children's connection to nature and naturalistic spaces such as forest schools, forest kindergartens, woodland camps, and nature kindergartens. The creation of a series of nature-based curriculum planning books has brought together her two areas of expertise.

Claire's unique approach to planning with and for children, called Floorbooks®, increases child-led inquiries that are centred around the fascinations children find when they learn with nature. The three spaces of "inside", "outside", and "beyond" are mindfully linked to develop skills and confidence in a predominantly natural environment.

In addition to Claire's international and consultancy work, she runs a community interest company, Living Classrooms, through which the virtual nature school is being delivered. Additionally, she set up the International Association of Nature Pedagogy, a professional organization designed to promote and support all forms of nature-based education for children aged 3 - 8 years throughout the world. This includes forest kindergartens, forest schools, nature preschools, and nature kindergartens.

Claire's philanthropic work has had a significant impact around the world. She is part of a leadership group of consultants who make up the World Nature Collaborative, a working party of the World Forum Foundation. The purpose of the group is to develop a cohesive network and approach to experiential learning in outdoor spaces in a variety of climates. The nature collaborative brings together educators, landscape architects, environmentalists, and health workers to support a multidisciplinary approach to outdoor educational provision.

We encourage you to visit www.mindstretchers.academy to download the complimentary *Fascination Series Handbook* that will guide you on how to teach the course virtually and provide you with a shopping list and additional resources to assist you.

Connect with Claire at www.mindstretchers.academy to stay up to date with all of the books in the *Fascination Series* along with additional resources and training.

"The true value of this little gem of a book is that it respects the power of allowing children to have their own adventures, follow their own imaginations and make their own discoveries."~ Tim Gill

"An invaluable and inspirational resource, by an internationally recognized expert in her field, that beautifully illustrates the power of nature to amplify every dimension of learning." ~ Richard Louv